ADOPT ME!
DRESS YOUR PETS!

HARPER

An Imprint of HarperCollinsPublishers

© 2023 Adopt Me!™
Visit playadopt.me and join the fun!
*Ask a parent before going online.

UPL**I**FT
G A M E S

23 24 25 26 27 HRNT 10 9 8 7 6 5 4 3 2 1
Originally published in Great Britain 2023 by Farshore
First US edition, 2023

ONLINE SAFETY FOR YOUNGER FANS

Spending time online is great fun! Here are a few simple rules to help younger fans stay safe and keep the internet a great place to spend time:
- Never give out your real name – don't use it as your username.
- Never give out any of your personal details.
- Never tell anybody which school you go to or how old you are.
- Never tell anybody your password except a parent or a guardian.
- Be aware that you must be 13 or over to create an account on many sites. Always check the site policy and ask a parent or guardian for permission before registering.
- Always tell a parent or guardian if something is worrying you.

Stay safe online. Any website addresses listed in this book are correct at the time of going to print. However, Farshore is not responsible for content hosted by third parties. Please be aware that online content can be subject to change and websites can contain content that is unsuitable for children. We advise that all children are supervised when using the internet.

FSC
www.fsc.org
MIX
Paper | Supporting
responsible forestry
FSC™ C007454

This book is produced from independently certified FSC™ paper
to ensure responsible forest management.

For more information visit: www.harpercollins.co.uk/green

WELCOME PARTY!

Join us in the wonderful world of Adopt Me! Collect amazing pets and dress them up. Find your favorite pets from the sticker pages and add some friends to make this a party!

STARTING OUT

When you first enter Adopt Me you will be given an egg that will hatch either a Dog or a Cat. Find the Starter Egg from your sticker sheet and then dress up these starter pets!

Place a Starter Egg sticker here

DOG
Starter pets are free when you start your game, but you can also trade for or buy this super-cute pup!

CAT
This little whiskered pal bounces on its feet while idle.

MINI MASTERPIECE

Draw the starter pet you receive here and add some accessories!

MAKE IT NEON

When you have four fully grown pets of the same kind, you can take them to the Neon Cave and brighten them up! Make these pets neon by coloring in different parts of their bodies using bold colors.

CREATURE CODE

Answers on page 32

Use your skills to find the names of four Legendary pets. Fill in the missing numbers in the grid and use them to crack the codes below.

A	B	C	D	E	F	G	H	I
		24					19	

J	K	L	M	N	O	P	Q	R
	16							

S	T	U	V	W	X	Y	Z
8		6			3		

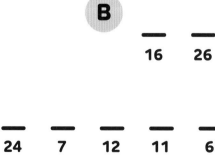

A

_	_	_	**A**	_	_	_
20	18	9	26	21	21	22

B

_	_	_	_	_	_	**R**	_	_
16	26	13	20	26	9		12	12

C

_	_	_	_	_	_	**S**
12	24	7	12	11	6	8

D

K	_	_	_	_	_	_
16	18	7	8	6	13	22

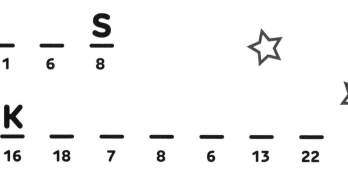

DRESS-UP DILEMMA

The pets' dress-up accessories are all mixed up! Use your stickers to sort them out and solve these puzzles. Each item must appear only once in each row, column or box. Good luck!

Easy

Key

Hard

Key

Answers on page 32

COMMON PETS

You should have no trouble adding these pets to your collection! Buy eggs or trade for these Common creatures. Dress them up with your adorable stickers and make them yours!

WALRUS
This wintery pet has glowing blue tusks when they become neon!

BULLFROG
When idle, the Bullfrog wobbles like jelly!

BANDICOOT
You will need to find just the right Aussie Egg for this Australian cutie!

UNCOMMON PETS

There are more types of Uncommon pets than Common pets to collect, but you might have to try a bit harder to obtain one. Give these pets a silly hat or a pair of glasses to have them feelin' good!

STEGOSAURUS
This cute prehistoric pet hatches from a Fossil Egg.

CRAB

Watch out for this pet's large red snapping claws! A cute little devil for sure!

FENNEC FOX

Dance with me! This cuddly creature loves dancing when fully grown.

RARE PETS!

Who doesn't want a pet that no one else has? If you can acquire these rarities you will have a collection that will really impress your friends. Don't forget to accessorise them!

COW
Common in the field, but a rare find in Adopt Me – get a Farm Egg to claim this moo-tastic pet!

RHINO

The Rhino is one of seven pets that you can find inside a Jungle Egg, making them an Eggcellent pet to have!

NARWHAL

The unicorn of the sea, this Ocean Egg pet has a large tusk on its head.

EGG MANIA!

A special event has started and there are many eggs up for grabs! Count how many of each egg type there are and add a star sticker when you have counted them all.

Place a star sticker here

Answers on page 32

SAFARI SHADOWS

These hatchlings can be found in Safari Eggs. Circle the matching shadow for each pet and add a sticker when you're done.

Place a Safari Egg sticker here

Elephant

A   B   C

Flamingo

A   B   C

Giraffe

A   B   C

Hyena

A   B   C

Answers on page 32

LEGENDARY RACE

Grab some players and see who can get to the Winged Horse first.

YOU WILL NEED:
- 2-4 players
- Something to act as counters
- A die

START →

1

2

3

12

Anything can happen. Move to the same square as the player on your left.

11

10

13

14

15

24

23

A Legendary find. Move forward 3 spaces.

22

25

26

27

HOW TO PLAY:
Place the counters on square 1, then take turns rolling the die and following the instructions as you go. The first to the FINISH square wins!

You've hatched a mmon pet. Miss a turn.

4

5

6

9

8

A Legendary find. Move forward 3 spaces.

7

You've hatched a Common pet. Miss a turn.

16

17

18

21

20

19

28

Anything can happen. Move to the same square as the player on your left.

29

FINISH →

30

19

ULTRA-RARE PETS!

These pets are hard to come by, but if you can find someone to trade you one you will be very lucky! Give these elusive creatures a makeover with your super-cool and rad accessory stickers.

SPACE WHALE
When this pet goes mega neon, its fins flash the colors of the rainbow!

WYVERN
Hatch this magical creature from a Mythic Egg. Time to spread your wings!

PUFFIN
This cute little bird glows cyan if you make it neon!

LEGENDARY PETS

These are the hardest pets to find in the entire game! Mythical, magical or just plain adorable, these pets are very satisfying to collect. Dress them up with your stickers.

UNICORN
Oh happy day! This was one of the very first Legendary pets in the game.

SHADOW DRAGON
Look out for this pet at night, when its tongue glows!

FALLOW DEER
Find this happy hopping creature in a Woodland Egg!

SPOT THE DIFFERENCE

It's time for an Adopt Me! pet party! Spot all 10 differences between these two pictures, adding a star sticker for every difference you find.

Place a star sticker here for each difference you find.

Answers on page 32

SPEEDY SCENE

There are so many cool, silly and rare vehicles in town. Add stickers of your favorite cars, bikes, boats, helicopters and more!

HAPPY HOUSE

You've got your own house and now it's time to decorate! Find your favorite furniture items on the sticker pages and make this house ready for all your adorable pets!

PET PUZZLE

Test your skills with this awesome word search! Find the names of these popular pets in the grid. They may be found written forwards, backwards or diagonally.

N	A	B	G	N	A	R	W	H	A	L	S	T	I	B	U
R	N	O	E	Y	B	T	O	O	R	A	G	N	A	K	M
E	R	I	A	C	M	O	N	S	E	A	H	O	R	S	E
V	O	H	R	A	A	T	M	A	H	Y	C	T	D	Z	R
Y	C	Q	E	M	L	T	K	R	H	I	N	O	E	E	A
W	I	E	F	T	B	E	J	B	M	P	D	T	C	B	B
T	N	F	Y	A	D	R	A	F	O	E	E	O	D	O	G
F	U	T	W	G	T	O	E	N	L	E	A	L	N	H	W
X	N	O	G	A	R	D	W	O	D	A	H	S	E	N	S

- [ ] CAT
- [ ] DOG
- [ ] OTTER
- [ ] KANGAROO
- [ ] UNICORN
- [ ] SHADOW DRAGON
- [ ] COW
- [ ] RHINO
- [ ] NARWHAL
- [ ] SEAHORSE
- [ ] ELEPHANT
- [ ] LAMB
- [ ] WYVERN

30

Answers on page 32

EGG MAZE

Make your way through the eggs from the START to the FINISH. Follow the below pattern in the exact order only.

START →

Follow the eggs in this order

FINISH →

ANSWERS

PAGE 8
A - GIRAFFE, B - KANGAROO,
C - OCTOPUS, D - KITSUNE

PAGE 9

EASY

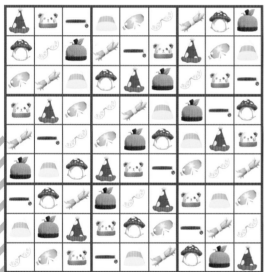

HARD

PAGE 16

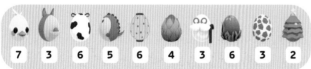

7	3	6	5	6	4	3	6	3	2

PAGE 17
ELEPHANT - B, FLAMINGO - A,
GIRAFFE - B, HYENA - C

PAGE 24-25

PAGE 30

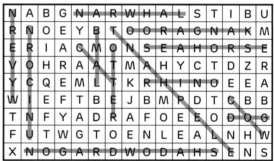

N	A	B	G	N	A	R	W	H	A	L	S	T	I	B	U
R	N	O	E	Y	B	T	O	O	R	A	G	N	A	K	M
E	R	I	A	C	M	O	N	S	E	A	H	O	R	S	E
V	O	H	R	A	A	T	M	A	H	Y	C	T	D	Z	R
Y	C	Q	E	M	L	T	K	R	H	I	N	O	E	E	A
W	I	E	F	T	B	E	J	B	M	P	D	T	C	B	B
T	N	F	Y	A	D	R	A	F	O	E	E	O	D	O	G
F	U	T	W	G	T	O	E	N	L	E	A	L	N	H	W
X	N	O	G	A	R	D	W	O	D	A	H	S	E	N	S

PAGE 31

32